Worship in Islam

Mustafa Ahmad Al-Zarqa

THE ISLAMIC FOUNDATION
United Kingdom - Kenya - Nigeria

Second Revised Edition 1977/1397 A.H.
Third Revised Edition 1980/1400 A.H.

ISBN 0 86037 008 9

Published by:
THE ISLAMIC FOUNDATION
223 London Road,
Leicester, LE2 1ZE,
United Kingdom.
Tel: (0533) 700725.

Quran House,
P.O. Box 30611,
Nairobi,
Kenya.

P.M.B. 3193,
Kano,
Nigeria.

Printed in England by:
JOSEPH BALL (Printers) LTD.,
72 Cannock Street,
Leicester
Tel: (0533) 740880

Worship in Islam

Worship, according to Islam, is a means for the purification both of man's soul and of his daily life.

The basis of *ʿibādah* (worship) is the fact that human beings are creatures and thus bond-servants of God, their Creator and their Lord, to Whom they are destined to return. Thus man's turning towards God, in intimate communion, reverence, and in the spirit of devotion and humble submission, is termed *ʿibādah.*

Worship is an indispensable part of all religions, including the idolatrous ones. However, in each religion, it is motivated by different objectives, assumes different forms and is performed under a different set of rules.

In some religions, worship is a means of developing in man an attitude of asceticism and isolation from life. In these religions it seeks to develop a mentality which anathematizes the enjoyment of the pleasures of this world.

Then, there are certain other religions which consecrate certain places for the sake of worship and prohibit its performance at any other place. There are also religions in which worship can be performed only under the leadership of a particular class of people—the ordained priests. Thus the nature and forms of worship differ from one religion to another.

Dr. Mstafa Ahmad Al-Zarqa is Professor of Islamic Law at the University of Jordan, Amman, and is a former Minister of Justice, Government of Syria. The article was originally published in Arabic in *al-Muslimūn,* Beirut. It has been translated by Dr. Zafar Ishaq Ansari, Associate Professor of Islamic Studies, University of Petroleum and Minerology, Dahran.

As for Islam, its conception of worship is related to its fundamental view that the true foundations of a good life are soundness of belief and thinking, purity of soul and righteousness of action.

Through belief in the Oneness of God, Who has all the attributes of perfection, Islam seeks to purge human intellect of the filth of idolatry and superstitious fancies. In fact, both polytheism and idolatry, which are opposed by Islam, degrade man to a level which is incompatible with his dignity. Islam fights against idolatry and polytheism in whatever forms and to whatever extent they may be found. In its concern to eradicate idolatry, Islam takes notice even of its imperceptible forms. It takes notice even of those beliefs and practices which do not appear to their adherents to be idolatrous. One of the manifestations of this concern is that Islam does not permit the performance of ritual prayer *(ṣalāh)* in front of a tomb, nor does it permit man to swear in the name of anyone except God. All this shows the uncompromising hostility of Islam to idolatry. When the Caliph ʿUmar saw that people had begun to sanctify the tree beneath which the Companions of the Holy Prophet (peace be upon him) had pledged to lay down their lives in the way of God on the occasion of Hudaybiyah, he feared that its sanctification might corrupt the beliefs of the people. He, therefore, had it cut down. By destroying everything which might blur the distinction between the creature and the Creator, Islam brought man out of the darkness of superstition and ignorance into the full daylight of reality.

Thus the purpose of worship in Islam is to serve as a means to purge man's soul and his daily life of sin and wickedness. It has been so regulated as to suffice for the purpose of this purification, provided it is performed in true sincerity and sufficient care is taken to preserve its true spirit.

DISTINGUISHING FEATURES

The characteristic features of worship as propounded by Islam may be stated as the following:

Freedom from Intermediaries

First of all, Islam has liberated worship from the bondage of intermediaries between a man and his Creator. Islam seeks to create a direct link between a man and his Lord, thus rendering the intercession of intermediaries unnecessary.

Religious scholars in Islam, it may be pointed out, are neither intermediaries between man and God nor are they considered to be entitled to accept or reject acts of worship on behalf of God. In the sight of God, rather are they ordinary human beings who have been burdened with the additional duty of imparting knowledge to those who lack knowledge. They are deemed guilty if they hold it back from the seekers after knowledge. In other words, the Islamic *Sharīʿah* does not impose the domination of religious scholars on the rest of the people. The function of these scholars is merely to guide people in the right direction. This is amply borne out by what Allah said to the Holy Prophet:

> "Remind them, for you are but a remembrancer; you are not at all a warder over them."
>
> (The Qurʾān 88: 21-22)

The Prophet (peace be upon him) also addressed his own daughter Fāṭimah with the following words, which show that all human beings stand on a footing of complete equality before God:

> "O Fāṭimah, daughter of Muḥammad! I shall be of no help to you before Allah".

Not Confined to Specific Places

Secondly, Islam has not only liberated man's *ʿibādah* (worship) from the bondage of intermediaries; it has also liberated it from confinement to specific places. Islam regards every place—whether it is one's dwelling place, the back of an animal, the deck of a vessel on the surface of the sea, or a mosque specifically built for worship—as pure enough for the performance of worship. Wherever a man may be, he can turn towards his Lord and enter into communion with Him. The Holy Prophet has expressed this idea beautifully:

> "The (whole of the) earth has been rendered for me a Mosque: pure and clean".

All-Embracing View

Thirdly, Islam has also considerably widened the scope of worship. In Islam, worship is not confined to specific prayers and litanies which are to be performed on particular occasions. Rather, Islam considers every virtuous action which has been performed sincerely and with a view to carrying out the commandments of God and in order to seek His Pleasure, an act of worship for which the man will be rewarded. Even eating, drinking, sleeping and enjoyment of innocent recreation, even those worldly actions which satisfy man's physical needs and even yield sensual pleasure, become acts of worship provided they are performed with true religious motives. Yes, even those acts become acts of worship if the intention underlying them is to comply with the Will of God: that is, if one tries to satisfy one's needs within legitimate means so as to keep oneself in check against indulging in things which are prohibited. It is also an act of worship to try to strengthen one's body by providing it with its due of nourishment and sleep; by making it undertake exertion as well as giving it rest and recreation so as to enable it to shoulder the responsibilities which have been placed on man by God. In fact, if one does all that with the intention of pleasing God, one's action is in harmony with the following saying of the Holy Prophet (peace be upon him):

> "A believer who is possessed of strength is better and dearer to God than a believer who is weak".

In short, it is simply by purification of motives that the actions which are part of worldly life become acts of devotion and worship.

Thus, it is possible for a man to advance spiritually even while he is fully enjoying the pleasures of worldly life. The reason is that during all this enjoyment his heart will be in communion with God by virtue of the purity of his intentions, and owing to his having bound himself completely to the service of God. It will enable him to remain perpetually in a state of submission, obedience and devotion to God—even during his working pursuits—and this is the very essence of worship.

For Islam, unlike some religions, does not anathematize gratification of man's instinctive bodily appetites.

Islam does not even consider abstention from the satisfaction of these desires to be in any way an act of greater piety and virtue than satisfying them. Islam wants man to enjoy the pleasures and good things of life provided he does not transgress the limits of legitimacy or the rights of others, nor trample upon moral excellence, nor injure the larger interests of his society.

There is a profound wisdom and an important reason for this extension of the scope of worship. The reason is that Islam wants a man's heart to remain in perpetual communion with his Lord. Islam also wants a man to observe ceaseless vigilance over his desires so that his life may become a source of his welfare in the life to come as the Qur'ān says:

> "Seek a home in the Hereafter through whatever God has given to you and neglect not your share in this world".
>
> (28: 77)

Now, when a person knows that even his enjoyments and pleasures can become acts of worship merely by virtue of purity of intention and motive, it becomes easy for him to render obedience to God continually and to direct all his attention to seeking Divine pleasure. For he knows well that this devotion to God does not necessarily mean abandonment of worldly life, and misery and wretchedness.

What does good intention lead to? It prevents man from forgetting God because of excessive self-indulgence. The Holy Prophet has said that (even) when a person affectionately puts a piece of food in the mouth of his wife in order to strengthen bonds of matrimonial love, he is rewarded for it. This is understandable for he is trying to fulfil the purpose of living together with love and affection, the purpose which, as the Qurʾān says, is the *raison d'étre* of family life.

> "Among His signs is that He has created spouses for you from among yourselves so that you may console yourselves with them. He has planted love and mercy between you".
>
> (30: 21)

INTENTION AND MOTIVE

Muslim jurists and scholars have proclaimed that good intention changes acts of habit *(ʿādah)* into acts of worship *(ʿibādah)*. Good intention creates a world of difference in human life. It is owing to the absence of purity of intention that there are people who eat and drink and satisfy their animal desires and while so doing they simply live on the same plane as the animals do. The reason for this is that their actions are actuated by no other motive than the gratification of animal desires. On the other hand, there are also people who are, apparently, similar to the aforementioned people in so far as they also satisfy their desires and enjoy the pleasures of life, but, thanks to the noble intention which motivates their actions, even their physical self-fulfilment becomes an act of worship for which they merit reward. The reason is that the motive behind all their actions is to live in compliance with the Will of God. Their sublimity of motive becomes manifest in their conduct in day-to-day life in so far as it reflects the fact that they distinguish between good and evil.

On the contrary, those whose lives are shorn of good intentions are liable to be overwhelmed by their lusts and are likely to slide into a life of sin and moral decadence. But purity of intention and high thinking tend, in people of the second category, to stand in the way of their slipping into degradation. And thanks to the positive attitude of Islam towards life, all this is ensured without depriving man of a wholesome enjoyment of life. The real basis of this difference lies in the fact that while the one is always mindful of God and remembers Him, the other is altogether negligent. It is this that makes the former a pious, worshipful being, and the latter a heedless, self-indulgent animal. It is for people of this kind that the Holy Qur'ān has said:

> "Those who disbelieve take their comfort in this life and eat even as the cattle eat, and the Fire is their habitation".
>
> (47: 12)

What a great loss then do people suffer by not rectifying their orientation of life and purifying their intentions. For it is this alone which transforms even their pursuits of pleasure and enjoyment into acts of worship. What a tragedy that people spoil the prospects of their eternal life although they could have been attained so easily, without necessarily losing their share in this world.

This is the Islamic philosophy of worship. Without saying "no" to any of man's legitimate physical needs and desires, Islam seeks to elevate humanity to a place which befits its dignity and status.

PURPOSE OF SPECIFIC RITUALS

The wide jurisdiction of worship—i.e. its incorporation of all acts which are performed with the intention of complying with the Will of God, including fulfilment of legitimate pleasure, is sometimes used as a pretext to support the erroneous view that the obligatory rituals for worship such as prayers, fasting, *zakāh* and pilgrimage can be dispensed with;

or that they are not very important. The truth, however, is quite contrary to this. In Islam, they are the chief means for strengthening man's attachment to God. Thus absolutely misconceived is the view of those who are given to laxity in religious matters with regard to the obligatory acts of worship, and imagine that true faith does not consist of *ṣalāh* (prayers) and *ṣawm* (fasting); that the basis of true faith is merely purity of heart, goodness of intention and soundness of conduct. This constitutes misrepresentation of Islamic teachings.

The intention to live a life of righteousness does not lend itself to external observation. Hence the mere intention to do good does not mark off the true man of faith from the rest. Religion must have an external aspect as well as an internal aspect.

This deliberate disregard of ritual obligations is destructive of the very foundations of religion. For, were that viewpoint to be adopted, everyone, even those who are in fact opposed to religion, could claim to be the devoutest of all worshippers! The prayers and all other prescribed forms of worship serve to distinguish those who really do have faith and wish sincerely to serve God from those who are content with lip-service. So important indeed is prayer that the Prophet has said: "*Ṣalāh* (prayer) is the Pillar of the Islamic religion, and whosoever abandons it, demolishes the very Pillar of religion".

A PRACTICAL IDEAL

The real purpose of Islam in declaring that *ʿibādah* (worship) embraces the total life of man is to make religious faith play a practical and effective role in reforming human life, in developing in man an attitude of dignified patience and fortitude in the face of hardships and difficulties and in creating in him the urge to strive for the prevalence of good and extirpation of evil.

All this makes it amply evident that Islam, the standard-bearer of the above-stated concepts and ideals, is opposed to those defeatist and isolationist philosophies which scholars have termed asceticism, that is, that erroneous kind of asceticism which is based on renunciation of the world, on resignation from the resources of life, on withdrawal from the life of action and struggle, on sheer stagnation and decadence. These attitudes have nothing to do with Islam. Rather, they are the symbols of defeatism and escape from the struggle of life. For life requires strength, material resources and active habits. The role of Islam in the struggle of life is a positive one. It is through this attitude that Islam ensures the channelling of man's powers and resources in such a manner as to lead eventually to general good. The Islamic system of worship is a means of ensuring this soundness of orientation.

An event may be narrated here to illustrate the Islamic attitude to the question under discussion, and to disabuse minds of wrong notions of what the spiritual life means. It is reported that ʿĀʾishah, the mother of the faithful, once saw a person walking with his body stooped down and his back bent with weakness, appearing as if he were not fully alive, attracting thereby the glances of those around him. She inquired about him and was informed that he was a saintly person. ʿĀʾishah denounced this kind of saintliness and said: 'Umar son of Khaṭṭāb, was the saintliest of people. But when he said something, he made himself heard; when he walked, he walked fast; and when he beat, his beating caused pain. Thus, to be more spiritual inwardly should make us more forthright and strong in the world.

طبع بتصريح وزارة الاعلام
رقم ٥٨٥٨ م ج
بتاريخ ١٤١١/٩/٨ هـ